Introduction

Ephesians In-Depth Bible Study
Walk by the Spirit

Thank you so much for reading this book. I understand that there are other study guides available, so I really do appreciate you taking the time to read mine. As for this book, I give all the glory to God. Without Him, this wouldn't be possible.

You may notice that some passages were skipped, this is because I did not feel it on my heart to touch base on them. Therefore, there will be some gaps.

Throughout this study, when I refer to the enemy, I always use a lowercase letter, even if it's the first word in the sentence. I know that it may sound odd, considering we are taught not to do this, but this was intentional. So often we give the enemy power in our lives. Through anxiety, fear, depression, or whatever else it is that you are going through. I wanted to show you that he has no hold on a child of God. So when you see these "grammar issues", know that they were done on purpose. Use them as a reminder that satan has no hold on you. In the name of Jesus, you don't belong to him. You are God's, and God's alone.

Ephesians 1:1-2

If you notice, when Paul writes his letters, I see the words *Grace to you and peace from God our Father and the Lord Jesus Christ*. It's nice to see that one of the very first things he said was a blessing to someone other than himself. I also notice words he says about himself, *an apostle of Jesus Christ by the will of God*, *bondservants of Jesus Christ*, etc. Seeing this, I can see that the letters are started with the knowledge that he knows who he is in Christ. He knows that he is who he is, because of God and God alone. He also knows that he is but a servant of the Lord. I believe this is a good thing, because it not only shows others how to behave, but also reminds himself who he is in Christ. Do you remember who you are in Christ? You would be quick to say yes, but do you really? Do you know how valuable you are as a child of God, how loved you are? Do you realize that whatever place you are in, at this very moment of your life, it's because God has allowed it? Do you realize that if you have kids, it's because God has entrusted them to you? Whatever place you are in, if you are following God's will, then you have to trust your journey. Grow where you have been planted, because wherever God has placed you, it's for a reason. I want to add that sometimes God asks us to do something, and when we do it, we wonder why things are not changing. We wonder why we did what He asked, but it seems like an even bigger mess than before. Take heart and be strengthened, because God knows exactly what He is doing. Sometimes the promise comes before the blessing. Look at David's journey. David was anointed to be king, yet the promise came before the blessing. David was anointed by Samuel to be king, but that promise came way before all of the many trials that he endured, it came, before the blessing. So you may wonder why you have not received the promise yet, but I assure you that it's coming. You need to be prepared first, but the blessing is coming. The promise is coming. Be patient and wait for it, it will not tarry. God has a plan and He knows exactly what He is doing. Worship in the waiting, read the word in the waiting, prepare yourself, in the waiting. Prepare yourself, so that whatever God has you do, you will be ready. I want to clarify, that God doesn't call the equipped, He equips the called. So I am not saying that you have to be ready for Him to call you, but what I am saying is that while you are waiting for the promise, while you are waiting for the blessing, don't sit idle. For example, if God tells you that He wants you to be a speaker, and you have a period of waiting until that happens, don't just sit and do nothing. Read the word, study the word, pray, and praise. Why? Because when the time comes, you will have the knowledge that comes during the waiting period. You will grow up in your faith and in your trust in the Lord. You will learn patience. You will learn whatever it is that God is trying to teach you in this waiting period. It may be different for one person than it is to the next. Only God knows the areas in your life that you need to work on. He knows you better than even you know yourself. This can work for anything. Let's say that you are waiting on the blessing of a child. Maybe God is preparing you for that child, maybe God wants you to get closer to Him first, so you can be a more Godly mother and raise your child with a good foundation, because maybe He has certain plans for that child too, and He needs to prepare you first, or maybe, God has a different path all together for you. Your womb is not what makes you a woman. Having kids does not make you who you are, and it sure doesn't define how God sees you. Being barren doesn't mean that you lose your purpose, no, it just means that you have a different route to take, and only God knows the why and the where, so trust Him. With all your heart, trust Him.

So remember, if you are waiting for the promise, don't sit idle.

Also, remember what I said in the beginning of this entry. Remember who you are in Christ. We are servants of the Lord. We are not our own. We were bought with a price.

Or do you not know that your body is the temple of the Holy Spirit who is in you, whom you have from God, and you are not your own? For you were bought at a price; therefore glorify God in your body and in your spirit, which are God's.

1 Corinthians 6:19-20

And certainly never forget how loved you are.

Ephesians 1:3-4

He is again acknowledging who God is. That He is the one who blessed them with every spiritual blessing in the heavenly places in Christ. He also states something that should remind you of who you are in Christ. God chose you before this world even came to be. Before He even laid its foundation, you were already chosen. Think about this for a second. God knows all, and He knew every mistake that you would make in life, He knew every wrong turn, and every mess up, but, He still chose you. Some people go through life thinking that they have to earn God's love, or that God won't love them because they made too many mistakes in life. Guess what? God knew that you would make those mistakes before you even made them, before you were even born! And yet, He still loved you enough to die for you, He still loved you enough to create you, and He still wanted you. If God knew all of the mistakes that you would make in life, but He still chose you to be born, doesn't that tell you something? Doesn't that tell you how truly loved you are? You don't need to be perfect for God to love you, because we will never be perfect. While on this earth, we will fail and we will fall, but the good news is, Jesus died for us, and because of that sacrifice, this life is temporary. It's temporary pain, for an eternal reward. A reward that we don't even deserve. So please, don't question if God loves you, or how can He ever love you, because He will always love you, regardless of what you think or feel. He will always love you with a perfect love.

Who shall separate us from the love of Christ? Shall tribulation, or distress, or persecution, or famine, or nakedness, or peril, or sword? As it is written:

"For Your sake we are killed all day long;
We are accounted as sheep for the slaughter."

Yet in all these things we are more than conquerors through Him who loved us. For I am persuaded that neither death nor life, nor angels nor principalities nor powers, nor things present nor things to come, nor height nor depth, nor any other created thing, shall be able to separate us from the love of God which is in Christ Jesus our Lord.

Romans 8:35-39

You were made to conquer. You were made to overcome this world, just as Jesus did.

"I have told you these things, so that in me you may have peace. In this world you will have trouble. But take heart! I have overcome the world."

John 16:33

Don't underestimate the power of Christ in you. You can overcome this world, because you are not fighting it alone.

For whatever is born of God overcomes the world. And this is the victory that has overcome the world—our faith. Who is he who overcomes the world, but he who believes that Jesus is the Son of God?

1 John 5:4-5

Remember, before you were even born, God chose you to be His. Not because He had to, but because He wanted to. Because of His great love for you. Don't doubt the love that He has already shown you He has for you.

Ephesians 1:5

God has not only predestined you to be His child through Christ Jesus, but He also predestined a plan for you. He has an exact plan for you, specific to you. Now whether you follow that plan or not, is completely up to you, but I assure you, your plan or anyone's plan for that matter, could never even compare to His. You can't see ahead, but He can. You don't know what path is best for you, but He does. You may think you want something on the path all the way to the left, but He actually wants something better for you, that's all the way on the right. You could be so set on something, so sure about something, and then God take you in a completely different direction. Think about it this way. God created you, and God knit you in your Mother's womb. God knew you before you were even born, before you even came to be, He knew you. He sees your past, your present, and your future.

How could anyone ever compare to the knowledge of God? The wisdom, the understanding, and the plans that He has for you? No one ever could. He can't be compared to anyone or anything. He is literally in His own field. None before, and none after. No one has, is, or ever will come close to being like Him. God knows exactly what He is doing with you, even in the painful moments, He knows. He has a specific plan for you. I urge you to take heart, follow God, and don't give up. He knows exactly what He is doing, even if you can't see it yet. In time, you will. Remember,

He has made everything beautiful in its time. Also He has put eternity in their hearts, except that no one can find out the work that God does from beginning to end.

Ecclesiastes 3:11

<u>Ephesians 1:5-6</u>

It was God's will, His joy, and His good pleasure, to make you His. He graciously made us His because we are accepted and beloved. Beloved means dearly loved. He doesn't just love you, He dearly loves you. Meaning you are not just a passing thought in His mind. He really and truly does love you, as a perfect Father loves you. As you see, I said <u>perfect</u> Father. I said this so you don't get caught up comparing Him to an earthly father, because as we know, those are not perfect. He's not anywhere near an earthly father, instead, He is a perfect, loving,

<u>heavenly</u> Father. There is no dad on earth that could ever compare to Him. No one who would love you as much, care for you as much, protect you as much, etc. Don't get caught up comparing Him to an earthly dad, because you would fall extremely short on how good God actually is. He loves you, dearly and perfectly, and He thinks about you more than you realize.

How precious also are Your thoughts to me, O God!
How great is the sum of them!
If I should count them, they would be more in number than the sand;
When I awake, I am still with You.

Psalms 139:17-18

Remember, God didn't choose you based on how perfect you are, He chose you, because He dearly loves you.

Ephesians 1:5

God predestined us to adoption as sons by Jesus Christ to Himself. Predestined means

(of an outcome or course of events) determined in advance by divine will or fate.

This means that God willingly determined in advance, before the world began, He willingly in advance made the path for all of us who choose to follow Jesus Christ, to become His children. He didn't do this out of need, but want. As we know, God is God, He doesn't need anything from us.

And he is not served by human hands, as if he needed anything. Rather, he himself gives everyone life and breath and everything else.

Acts 17:25

What I find interesting is that next verse in Acts.

From one man he made all the nations, that they should inhabit the whole earth; and he marked out their appointed times in history and the boundaries of their lands.

Acts 17:26

So if you couple together that God chose you before He even made the earth, and this verse in Acts 17:26, we can clearly see that not only did God chose you to be His, but He also set you exactly where you are in this very moment of your life, for a reason. The place you were born, and the time you were born, all set by God.

I want to add that if you are following God's path, and you know that it's the right path, but it seems so dark, you have to understand something. All paths may seem dark at the moment, but there is only one path that God is on. What I mean is this. You may have multiple paths to take, but there is only one that God is trying to turn you towards. The other paths are not His paths. There is only one path that you are meant to be on, and that's God's path.

I also want you to remember something. Sometimes you have to be willing to be in the storm, in order to help others through that storm. For example, if you are on a path that God wants you on, and it's really difficult, painful, and sorrowful, then you are gaining faith, wisdom, clarity, etc, for the next person who goes down that road. To clarify a little more for you, I have dealt with anxiety for years now. I have gotten so much better, but I also know that there is still work to do. I could choose to give up, and never leave the house again, or, I can choose to be in this storm, fight with every ounce I have, overcome it, and help others with the same or similar issues. I have chosen to be in the storm. When you choose the harder path, you will realize that the narrow path, really is narrow. It's so hard at times, it's so sorrowful at times, but I also find joy, hope, peace, love, and a Father who cares deeply for me. No where in the scriptures did God say that life would be easy for us. In fact, we can see throughout the scriptures, that we actually suffer. So we're not told that anything would be easy, but we are told that He is with us. With us through the pain, the suffering, the anxious moments, and all the rest. And yes, you can do all things through Christ who strengthens you, but don't misunderstand the text. I am referring to the verse in Philippians 4:13 that says, "*I can do all things through Christ who strengthens me.*" If you look at the context before this verse, it clearly states what he meant.

I am not saying this because I am in need, for I have learned to be content whatever the circumstances. I know what it is to be in need, and I know what it is to have plenty. I have learned the secret of being content in any and every situation, whether well fed or hungry, whether living in plenty or in want. I can do all this through him who gives me strength.

Philippians 4:11-13

He is basically saying that yes, he has faced many trials, he has been well fed, but he has also been hungry, he has lived in plenty, and he has also lived in want, but, he has learned that no matter what situation he is in, and no matter what he faces, he has learned the secret to being content in all circumstances. The secret is that he can get through anything that he is faced with, because he is not alone. Because God gives him strength to keep fighting, to endure, and to press on. Therefore, he can do all things through Christ who gives him strength, and so can you. So if you are someone who likes hanging scriptures on walls, jewelry, etc, remember the meaning of this one. That no matter what it is you face in life, you can and you will get through it, because God will give you the strength to endure, through the good, and the bad. And remember, God works all things together for good, to those who love Him. He works ALL things together for good. This means the good and the bad.

And we know that all things work together for good to those who love God, to those who are the called according to His purpose.

Romans 8:28

And yes, if you believe in the death and resurrection of Jesus Christ, and if you follow Christ and believe that He is Lord, then yes, you are called. And yes, you do have a good purpose.

Ephesians 1:7

We have redemption through Jesus, and through Jesus alone. YOU CAN NOT GET TO THE FATHER WITHOUT THE SON. If you are someone who believes that you can, you are sadly mistaken. You NEED Jesus.

Whoever denies the Son does not have the Father either; he who acknowledges the Son has the Father also.

1 John 2:23

If you are living any other way, then you need to re-evaluate. You need to realize that you can't get to the Father, without the Son. Jesus is part of the Trinity. The Father, the Son, and the Holy Spirit. All God, all equally important. All three are FULLY God, not separate, and no, One doesn't have more God than the Other. They are all equally God, and all 3 are the same God. They are <u>NOT</u> three different gods.

I know this may sound confusing, so I put this picture below to best describe the Trinity.

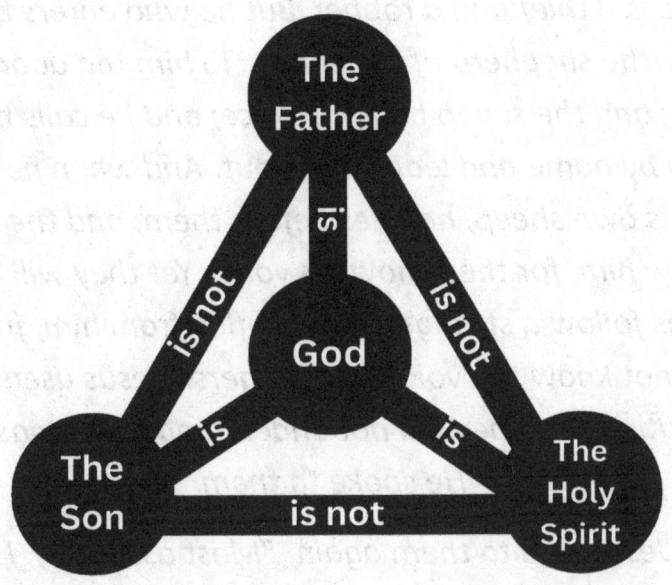

I also want to point something out. If you believe that you have been saved, and you only believe in God the Father, then how can you have redemption and forgiveness of sins? If you owe someone money, and I give you the money to pay off the debt, that means that without me, you are still in debt. A debt that you can not afford to pay. Remember to look closely at this verse in Ephesians 1:7. It clearly tells us that our redemption is through Jesus's blood. The forgiveness of our sins, is only found through Jesus's blood. This is what made our payment, and without that payment, we are still in debt. A debt that we can not afford to pay. If you try to go around Jesus, you are but a thief. You have to go through the Shepherds door, which is Jesus, and Jesus only.

Most assuredly, I say to you, he who does not enter the sheepfold by the door, but climbs up some other way, the same is a thief and a robber. But he who enters by the door is the shepherd of the sheep. To him the doorkeeper opens, and the sheep hear his voice; and he calls his own sheep by name and leads them out. And when he brings out his own sheep, he goes before them; and the sheep follow him, for they know his voice. Yet they will by no means follow a stranger, but will flee from him, for they do not know the voice of strangers." Jesus used this illustration, but they did not understand the things which He spoke to them.

Then Jesus said to them again, "Most assuredly, I say to you, I am the door of the sheep. All who ever came before Me are thieves and robbers, but the sheep did not hear them. I am the door. If anyone enters by Me, he will be saved, and will go in and out and find pasture. The thief does not come except to steal, and to kill, and to destroy. I have come that they may have life, and that they may have it more abundantly.

John 10:1-10

If you still at this point in your life, have not accepted Jesus as your Savior, I would strongly urge you that He is the only way in. You can not get to heaven by only knowing the Father, because if you don't know the Son, then you don't know the Father either. You also can not get to heaven by doing good works, and you certainly can not get to heaven by just walking in, without knowing Jesus Christ as your Savior. The bible clearly states how we are saved.

But what does it say? "The word is near you, in your mouth and in your heart" (that is, the word of faith which we preach): that if you confess with your mouth the Lord Jesus and believe in your heart that God has raised Him from the dead, you will be saved. For with the heart one believes unto righteousness, and with the mouth confession is made unto salvation. For the Scripture says, "Whoever believes on Him will not be put to shame."

Romans 10:8-11

All it takes, is for you to believe. Believe that Jesus is Lord, believe that Jesus died on the cross for your sins, and believe that God raised Him from the dead, then you will be saved. Life doesn't come easily for many. We have to work for things, and we have to do things for ourselves, because no one will help us, and the list goes on. But, this doesn't require any work on your end. You are literally being handed eternity with a loving God. All you have to do is believe. Believe with the faith that God is offering you to believe. You see, there is no part of your redemption that comes from you. Everything has literally been handed to you. The price was already paid for you, one that none of us deserve. It's waiting for you to just reach out and take it. If I hand you the money to pay off your debt, you would have to first reach out and accept that money. The same goes for this. You have to reach out and take the gift that you are being given. You have the choice to accept it, or reject it. I really hope that you make the right choice. I am placing a prayer below to help you along your way. I know sometimes it's hard to find the words to say, so I hope this helps.

Dear God, I come to You today asking You to forgive me of my sins. I believe and declare with my mouth that Jesus is Lord, and I believe that You died and rose again. I want to live my life for You. Lead me and guide me on the path that You have chosen for me. Even if it's hard God, I still want to follow You. Thank You for the sacrifice that you made for me. The price that You paid for me, so that one day, I can be with You for all eternity. Thank You for loving me that much, that You gave Your life for me. In Jesus name I pray, Amen.

If you prayed that prayer, then I am so proud of you! Following Jesus isn't always easy, but there is no better path to follow. I pray for all who are reading this book, to be strengthened on your journey. Life is hard, but walking through it with Jesus, makes it so much better.

Ephesians 1:13-14

The moment that you accepted and believed in Jesus Christ, is the moment that you were graciously given the

Holy Spirit of promise. The Holy Spirit is the guarantee of your inheritance, until we are safely seated in the heavenly places with Him. We are God's possession, purchased by the blood of Jesus Christ. As sons and daughters of the Most High, we have an inheritance. One that is undeserved, and one that God has so graciously bestowed upon us. How grateful I truly am for this.

Ephesians 1:15-21

Here we see that Paul is grateful for the faith of others, and the love that they show the saints. He is grateful for them, giving thanks to God for them, and mentioning them in his prayers. This is a perfect example of not only rejoicing in someones else's faith, but also rejoicing that they are showing Christ's love to others. This also shows us the importance of encouraging one another and lifting each other up, and it also shows us the importance of praying for others, not only when they are in need, but also when they are not. How great would the Ephesians have felt, knowing that someone was proud of them, thanking God for them, and lifting them up in their prayers? We too must show others the same encouragement. Not that we live for the encouragement of men, but it is still nice to know that someone cares.

We also see that not only is Paul thanking God for them, and commending their work in the Lord, but Paul is also praying for them to have wisdom, understanding, that they may know the hope of His calling, etc.

Paul wants them to know that the same power that worked in Christ, the same power that raised Christ from the dead, and seated Him at the right hand of God in the heavenly places, this same power, works toward us who believe. The same God who raised Jesus from the dead, is the same God who works in you. The same God who parted the sea, delivered His people from Egypt, and turned water to blood, is the same God who works in you. The same God who works in you, is the same God who is above all things. He is the same God who rules over all, created all, and is in control of all. This same God has all power and dominion over all things, and is at all places, at all times, and is present everywhere. I love this statement in this passage, because it reminds us of the Almighty God who is on our side. It reminds us that we have nothing to fear, because God is above all fear, depression, anxiety, etc. Who can be against us, when God is for us?

For those God foreknew he also predestined to be conformed to the image of his Son, that he might be the firstborn among many brothers and sisters. And those he predestined, he also called; those he called, he also justified; those he justified, he also glorified.

What, then, shall we say in response to these things? If God is for us, who can be against us?

Romans 8:29-31

Ephesians 1:22-23

God put all things under the feet of Jesus. Christ is the head over all things to the church, which is His body, the fullness of Him who fills all in all. This does not mean that if you don't go to church, you are not part of the body. The church does not have to be a physical place, but in fact, it is all believers. All believers are Christ's body, and He is the head of us all. We all fit together into one body, the body of Christ.

Ephesians 2:1-10

We who were once dead, were made alive in Christ. We once walked according to this world, according to satan, who is the prince of this world. The power of satan works in the sons of disobedience. We must remember, that his reign will come to an end. The people who follow this world, follow the lusts of the flesh, fulfill the desires of the flesh, and of the mind. These are children of wrath by nature. Remember, the enemy is not mindful of the things of God, but of the world.

However, our God who is rich in mercy, and because of how greatly He loves us, even when we were dead in our sins, made us alive together with Christ. It is by His grace that we have been saved. God made us raised up together with Christ in the heavenly places, that in the times to come, He might show the exceeding riches of His grace in His kindness toward us in Christ Jesus.

It is by grace through faith that we have been saved. We were not saved because of something that we said or did, but by grace, through faith. In this way, we can not boast, as if it was our works that have saved us. Instead, we know that it is a gift of God.

We are God's workmanship. We are God's work, made by His hands, and we were created in Christ Jesus for good works. These works He prepared for us before we were even born. These works were not prepared just to be prepared, but they were prepared so that we may walk in them.

God is the true Author of our story. We must try to stop writing the pages ourselves, but entrust ourselves to the One who knows what is best for us, and the One who already prepared our works for us. It is only our job to follow what He asks of us. We are not meant to clear our own path, but follow the one that God has already preordained for us to walk on. The question to ask yourself is, did I do what God asked me to do, or am I trying to clear my own path?

If you notice, Ephesians 2:10 says that we "*should*" walk in them. This signifies that we have a choice to follow what God has set before us or not. I for one, choose to obey, as God's ways are always higher and better than mine.

Ephesians 2:11-18

We were once separated from Christ. We had no hope and were without God. But, because of what Jesus did at the cross, we are now no longer far off, because we were brought near through the blood of Christ.

He is our peace, and where there was once a middle wall of separation, He broke down. There are no longer Jew and Gentile, circumcised and uncircumcised, but have now both been made one. We are no longer separated from God.

Jesus, who came down and took on the appearance of man in the flesh, utterly destroyed the separation that once was.

who, being in the form of God, did not consider it robbery to be equal with God, but made Himself of no reputation, taking the form of a bondservant, and coming in the likeness of men. And being found in appearance as a man, He humbled Himself and became obedient to the point of death, even the death of the cross.

Philippians 2:6-8

He destroyed the hostility that was once between us and God. Through His flesh, He abolished the hostility between us, and changed everything. We went from being under the law, to under grace. For who could uphold the whole law? Through Jesus Christ, God made peace with us. Therefore, through Jesus's body, and through His death on the cross, the hostility ended. When the hostility ended, there was peace. Peace not only between Jews and God, but Gentiles and God. Redemption was now offered to all who believed in His Son, regardless of heritage. Sacrifices no longer needed to be made, and we became children of God, receiving the promised Holy Spirit. Now this, is something to rejoice in.

Ephesians 2:19-22

Because of what Jesus did, we are no longer foreigners, no longer strangers. We are now fellow citizens with the saints and members of the household of God.

In older times, a cornerstone was used as the main stone in a building. It was usually the first one set, and all others were based off of the cornerstone. If the cornerstone was placed crooked, then it would affect the whole structure. The building could collapse, if not set correctly. The soundness of the building, relied on the placement of the cornerstone, as all the rest of the pieces, bore down on the cornerstone.

Jesus should be the first stone set in our foundation. He needs to be the main stone. You can't have Him second to another, or your building will collapse. If you set Him crooked, and only follow Him sometimes, your building again, collapses. Jesus is the One in whom you should set all of your other bricks upon. Meaning that everything you set in your life, should be built around Him. He needs to be the center of your life, your family, your work, etc. Everything that you do, should be done with Jesus in mind. For example, the way you treat your spouse, your kids, a co-worker, a friend, a parent, etc. It also means that when you work, you work as if it's for the Lord. Even if it's something simple like homework, do it as if it's for the Lord. Work wholeheartedly at all you do, as if it's for the Lord.

Remember, if you have neglected to set Jesus as your main stone, the cornerstone, your building will keep collapsing. It is not until you set Jesus first, that you will have a sturdy foundation.

This also reminds me of a scripture in Matthew.

"Therefore whoever hears these sayings of Mine, and does them, I will liken him to a wise man who built his house on the rock: and the rain descended, the floods came, and the winds blew and beat on that house; and it did not fall, for it was founded on the rock.
"But everyone who hears these sayings of Mine, and does not do them, will be like a foolish man who built his house on the sand: and the rain descended, the floods came, and the winds blew and beat on that house; and it fell. And great was its fall."

Matthew 7:24-27

If you don't have Jesus as your main stone, it's like building your house on sand, and it will eventually fall. You need to build upon Jesus Christ. He is the only solid Rock in which you should stand.

Remember, God dwells within you. The foundation that you are building, and the life that your living, is a dwelling place for the Holy Spirit, so live in a manner pleasing to the Lord.

Ephesians 3:1-7

Paul was graciously given the revelation of the gospel of Jesus Christ, through the Holy Spirit. What was once formerly a mystery to all people, was now made known to man, and Paul, was one of the ones chosen, to share this mystery. This mystery that was now made known, revealed that the Gentiles could be fellow heirs of this promise. The Gentiles are now of the same body, and we can all partake of God's promise that is in Jesus Christ. All believers are benefactors of this promise, regardless of who you are, or what your heritage is.

Here I am reminded that many people will be invited, but only a few chosen. God desires all to be saved, but there are so many who reject this truth, the truth of Jesus Christ. It saddens me because here we have a loving Father, who is gracious enough to invite us to His wedding feast, who wants all to come, but sadly enough, so many refuse Him. He is a Father who has so much love in His heart, that He wants all to know Him, but He faces the rejection of so many. He deserves so much love, yet, gets rejected over and over again. He invites many to the feast, but few are chosen.

Jesus spoke to them again in parables, saying: "The kingdom of heaven is like a king who prepared a wedding banquet for his son. He sent his servants to those who had been invited to the banquet to tell them to come, but they refused to come.

"Then he sent some more servants and said, 'Tell those who have been invited that I have prepared my dinner: My oxen and fattened cattle have been butchered, and everything is ready. Come to the wedding banquet.'

"But they paid no attention and went off—one to his field, another to his business. The rest seized his servants, mistreated them and killed them. The king was enraged. He sent his army and destroyed those murderers and burned their city.

"Then he said to his servants, 'The wedding banquet is ready, but those I invited did not deserve to come. So go to the street corners and invite to the banquet anyone you find.' So the servants went out into the streets and gathered all the people they could find, the bad as well as the good, and the wedding hall was filled with guests.

"But when the king came in to see the guests, he noticed a man there who was not wearing wedding clothes. He

asked, 'How did you get in here without wedding clothes, friend?' The man was speechless.

"Then the king told the attendants, 'Tie him hand and foot, and throw him outside, into the darkness, where there will be weeping and gnashing of teeth.'

"For many are invited, but few are chosen."

Matthew 22:1-14

Ephesians 3:8-12

Here Paul is saying that he is less than even the least of all the saints. Yes, God's grace extended to even him. One who persecuted God's people, one who did evil in the sight of God, now used by God, and by the grace of God, redeemed and forgiven. This grace was given to Paul, that he should preach to the Gentiles, Christ Jesus. That they may know what was once a mystery, now revealed through Christ Jesus, who through Him, all things were created.

I also want to point out, that in verse 12, we see that we have boldness and access with confidence, through Christ Jesus. If you are wondering how you can step out and do the thing that God has called you to do, if you are wondering how you can step out and preach the gospel to all nations, the answer is right here. You have boldness and direct access to Jesus Christ. The Holy Spirit will guide you and help you along the way, in whatever it is that God has called you to do. You don't have to be afraid, because it's not your strength and boldness that you are using, it's God's. If you don't have Christ Jesus, then you don't have this promise, but if you do, then you can do all things through Christ. That doesn't mean that they will be easy, but it does mean that you can do it. So if God is calling you to do something, step out. Moses questioned God over and over, and we see God's responses, showing Moses that He is with him. Moses's strength didn't matter, God's did. Look at David and Goliath. David's strength didn't matter, because God's did. God was with David, and that is what mattered. God wasn't with Goliath, but with David. God always wins. We clearly see this through the death and resurrection of Jesus Christ. God always accomplishes what He sets out to do.

For the LORD Almighty has purposed, and who can thwart him?
His hand is stretched out, and who can turn it back?

Isaiah 14:27

God never fails to rescue His children, protect His children, and love His children. That doesn't mean that the fight will be easy for you, but it does mean that He is with you. God would never call you to do something, and then leave your side. Whatever it is that God is calling you to do, do it, and He will be with you as you do.

No one can stop you from doing God's will, but you. Are you ready to keep fighting?

Ephesians 3:13

Here Paul is asking them not to lose heart at his tribulations. Paul recognizes that the trials he is facing, are not faced in vain. God has purposed them, and God has a plan for them. Not only did Paul's trials help people back then, but they still also bear witness to us today. This reminds me of a scripture in Acts.

About midnight Paul and Silas were praying and singing hymns to God, and the other prisoners were listening to them. Suddenly there was such a violent earthquake that the foundations of the prison were shaken. At once all the prison doors flew open, and everyone's chains came loose. The jailer woke up, and when he saw the prison doors open, he drew his sword and was about to kill himself because he thought the prisoners had escaped. But Paul shouted, "Don't harm yourself! We are all here!"

The jailer called for lights, rushed in and fell trembling before Paul and Silas. He then brought them out and asked, "Sirs, what must I do to be saved?"

They replied, "Believe in the Lord Jesus, and you will be saved—you and your household." Then they spoke the word of the Lord to him and to all the others in his house. At that hour of the night the jailer took them and washed their wounds; then immediately he and all his household were baptized. The jailer brought them into his house and

*set a meal before them; he was filled with joy because he
had come to believe in God—he and his whole household.*

Acts 16:25-34

So here we see that God used Paul's suffering. Because
Paul went to prison, he was able to bring this man and his
whole family to Jesus. His tribulations, turned out for
God's glory, and the benefit of others. We also see that
the prisoners were listening to Paul and Silas praying and
singing hymns to God. He was a light to those around
him, despite his tribulations. This is why it is so important
to respond correctly through tribulations. I know, it's not
easy. I can attest to how hard it can be to respond
correctly to trials sometimes. Things get overwhelming,
you get hit back to back to back, and things seem to
never let up. The fact is, the storm will pass, the trials will
pass, and everything you face, is temporary. You have to
realize that after these tribulations are over, all that you
will be left with, is how did you respond when you were
going through them? Did you do as Paul and Silas did
when they were in prison? Do you do as they did, and
even though they were in a trial, they were still praying
and singing hymns to God, or did you get led astray? Did
you worry, or did you give your pain to God? As I said, I
know how hard this is. Sometimes I get things right,
sometimes I don't, but the fact is, God knows that we are
human, and that we are but dust.

For He knows our frame;
He remembers that we are dust.

Psalm 103:14

Please take a moment to read all of Psalm 103

God is merciful and forgiving. God knows when you are trying, and when you are not. As long as you are trying your hardest to respond correctly, God notices that effort. And the times when you try and fail, God is gracious and merciful, and He forgives you. Listen, God knows your heart, and He knows those who are His, those who are for Him, and those who are trying to please Him. He is God, and He knows all. But I can attest to the fact that through those falls, those times when things get so overwhelming that you just break down, that God uses those times to grow your faith, your patience, your courage, your persistence, etc. We learn the most through the trials and the pain. If everything was going great, and your life was perfect, you wouldn't get to see God in action. You wouldn't get to see how He saves you, protects you, strengthens you, etc. So it's through these hard times, that you grow, and you get closer to God. You may not be able to see everything, but God does. God knows exactly what He is doing, so trust Him.

Trust in the LORD with all your heart
and lean not on your own understanding;
in all your ways submit to him,

and he will make your paths straight.

Proverbs 3:5-6

Ephesians 3:14

Here we see that Paul is praying. And it is so beautiful that he mentions us all as a family. The whole family of Christ. I think sometimes people forget that we are a family. Look at how all believers were one in heart.

All the believers were one in heart and mind. No one claimed that any of their possessions was their own, but they shared everything they had. With great power the apostles continued to testify to the resurrection of the Lord Jesus. And God's grace was so powerfully at work in them all that there were no needy persons among them. For from time to time those who owned land or houses sold them, brought the money from the sales and put it at the apostles' feet, and it was distributed to anyone who had need.

Joseph, a Levite from Cyprus, whom the apostles called Barnabas (which means "son of encouragement"), sold a field he owned and brought the money and put it at the apostles' feet.

Acts 4:32-37

A lot of people have forgotten that all believers are one in heart. We should be caring for each other, loving each other, forgiving each other, helping each other, praying for each other, etc. Jesus showed us by example, that we should be treating each other with love. We have come so far from since this was written, and not in a good way. Could you imagine someone selling land they own, just to help you with your needs? It's rarely heard of. We need to get back to the love that Jesus showed us. The love that He showed those around Him, leading to the ultimate sacrifice of love, through His death and resurrection. We have got to stop being so stingy with our possessions, and we have got to start loving one another the way we should. All the things on this earth are temporary. All those things that you are hoarding, will one day be left for someone else to take. Why not share it now? Why not share and glorify God on this earth while you can? If you only had 1 dollar left, and your child wanted it, would you give it to them? We should be willing to do the same for others as well. You may say that you don't own much to share, but there is always something to give. You can give your time, your love, your support, your prayers, etc. Sometimes the best gift that you could give someone, is a listening ear, words of encouragement, or an everything will be OK. Our family is so much bigger than the ones who surround us everyday. We would all be wise to remember that.

Ephesians 3:14-19

Here Paul is selflessly praying for others. He isn't praying for his own strength, but he is praying for the strength of others. That they would be strengthened with might through the Holy Spirit that dwells within them. He prayed that Christ may dwell in their hearts through faith, and that they, being rooted and grounded in love, may be able to comprehend with all of the saints, to know how far and how wide Christs love is for them. The love that surpasses all knowledge. This means that however much you think God loves you, you are so far off from how much He truly loves you. You could never even begin to comprehend the love that Christ has for you. It's too far, too wide to understand. He also prays that they be filled with all the fullness of God. I as well, pray this for you. Whoever is reading or hearing these words, I pray this prayer for you.

I also want to add that in verse 16, Paul is praying that He would grant them to be strengthened with might. The definition of might is

1 a: the power, authority, or resources wielded (as by an individual or group)
b(1): bodily strength
(2): the power, energy, or intensity of which one is capable

Examples
ran with all her might
striving with might and main

So here, Paul is not only praying for power for them, but he does it knowing that this power can't be found anywhere but in God, through Christ Jesus, and through the working of the Holy Spirit. This can never be done on our own. This power strengthens us inside. It gives us boldness, courage, might, importance, among many other things. But it is through God's grace, by faith, that this is even possible. In other words,

No Jesus = No faith and no might
Know Jesus = Faith and might

Ephesians 3:20-21

What is it that you are asking God for? I want you to always remember that God can do above and beyond all that we ask, think, or imagine. Sometimes, we look at things and think that our prayers are not being answered. What you have to realize is, sometimes when our prayers are answered, they are answered differently than we asked. For example, you may ask God for this job, but instead, He leads you to a different job. Only God knows the best way to answer your prayers. His thoughts and ways are higher than ours, and we have no clue a lot of the times, what's actually best for us. Therefore, we don't know what we ought to ask for, this is why we have the Holy Spirit's loving help.

Not only that, but we also who have the firstfruits of the Spirit, even we ourselves groan within ourselves, eagerly

waiting for the adoption, the redemption of our body. For we were saved in this hope, but hope that is seen is not hope; for why does one still hope for what he sees? But if we hope for what we do not see, we eagerly wait for it with perseverance.

Likewise the Spirit also helps in our weaknesses. For we do not know what we should pray for as we ought, but the Spirit Himself makes intercession for us with groanings which cannot be uttered. Now He who searches the hearts knows what the mind of the Spirit is, because He makes intercession for the saints according to the will of God.

And we know that all things work together for good to those who love God, to those who are the called according to His purpose.

Romans 8:23-28

"For my thoughts are not your thoughts,
neither are your ways my ways,"
declares the LORD.
"As the heavens are higher than the earth,
so are my ways higher than your ways
and my thoughts than your thoughts.

Isaiah 55:8-9

Remember, what you think you want God to do, and what's actually best for you, may be two completely opposite things. He is able to do above and beyond all that you ask, think, or imagine, through the working of power of the Holy Spirit who dwells within you.

Remember, the Maker always knows what's best for His creation.

Ephesians 4:1-6

We have two types of callings in life. One is personal, and God made it specifically for you, and one is universal, for all of His children. The personal calling is one that God has put a call on your life to do. Maybe it's a singer, a writer, a parent, a business owner, etc. Everyone of God's children has a personal calling from God. A personal calling can look different from one person to the next. Then, we have the universal calling. This calling is that all believers, as a whole, should follow Christ, forgive, love one another, build each other up, etc. I believe that this passage pertains to both the personal calling, and the universal one.

Ephesians 4:7

When Jesus died on the cross for us, it was more than enough. God gave us way more than we would ever deserve, by sending His One and Only Son to die for us. Yet, because God is so good, He still graciously gives. He gives us gifts, forgiveness, grace, mercy, love, comfort, answered prayers, etc. Isn't it so indescribably beautiful, the way He loves us?

Ephesians 4:11-13

Some people God calls to be apostles, some prophets, some evangelists, and some pastors and teachers.

Let's take a pastor for example. A pastor is meant to equip you for the work of ministry. When you hear a pastor preach, it's not meant to be heard, and then you go about your day. Instead, you are being equipped to do good works. The message is not just words, but an equipping. It's to equip you and to put what you were equipped with, to good use. Depending on the message the pastor is teaching, it can be used for things like teaching you patience, compassion, forgiveness, etc. This makes us more like Christ, if we choose to follow the teaching. It is also instructing you, so you are better equipped to instruct and help others as well. What I am trying to say is, don't just listen to a sermon and then discard it. Instead, put it to good use, and use it for good works through Jesus Christ.

Ephesians 4:14

Until the day that we are called home, we will keep having to work at being more like Christ. It is not until we are together with Him, that we will be fully like Him.

Beloved, now we are children of God; and it has not yet been revealed what we shall be, but we know that when He is revealed, we shall be like Him, for we shall see Him as He is.

1 John 3:2

But, as we grow and become more and more like Christ, learning to walk by the Spirit, and not the flesh, we will become steadfast, with Jesus as our anchor. When an anchor is thrown down into the ocean, it doesn't mean that the waves won't hit the boat, but what it does mean, is that it won't be moved by them. Why? Because your anchor is firm, secure, and nothing can move it. Jesus is your anchor. Jesus is unmovable, therefore, you become unmovable.

Ephesians 4:14

Instead of being tossed to and fro, with every gust of wind that comes your way, you are now grounded, built on a Rock. This Rock can not be moved, and you know who you are in Christ. This can't be done without faith. If you don't believe that Jesus can get you through whatever it is that you are going through, then the wind has moved you. If you allow others to sway your beliefs, then you have allowed the wind to move you. You must be firmly planted in Christ Jesus, to be unmovable. Now this doesn't mean that your boat won't rock from time to time, but what it does mean, is that it won't move. Your doubts will get crushed by the knowing of who your God is, and who you are in Him. You know full well that you are fully known, and that the One who fully knows you, has your back. He holds you up, and He guides your steps. He may allow you to get rocked, but He won't allow you to sink.

This, is faith. Believing that He can do all things, regardless of how big the winds and waves are. Believing that with God, all things truly are possible.

Remember, even though God may not deter what it is that you are going through, He will give you the strength to endure it.

Ephesians 4:15-16

Instead, we speak the truth with love, and in love. We grow up, becoming more and more like the One we are meant to be like, Christ Jesus, who is the head of us all. All believers are joined to Christ, us being the body, and Him as the head.

I want to point out, that here it says we are joined and knit together by what every joint supplies. This goes to show you, that we are meant to supply to the body of Christ. We are not meant to sit dormant. We are meant to be lights, not only to others who are far off from Christ, but also those who are in the body of Christ with us.

Just as we discussed in Ephesians 3:14, all believers were one in heart and mind. This was found in Acts 4:32-37.

We are meant to be effective, working together as a whole. Where one lacks, the other picks up, if one falls, we all help that one up, etc. This causes growth of the body for the edifying of itself in love. This helps us improve together as a whole, through the same love that we were taught by Christ Jesus.

Take a tree for example. If the branch needed nutrients, would the rest of the tree neglect to share its nutrients with that branch? Would the tree just allow it to die off, as if it meant nothing to begin with? For what is a tree without its branches? It is then a stump, good for nothing. Without branches, it can not grow fruit. How can that branch share the fruit, if it has none? In other words, we are the branches, and we all matter. If one needs to be uplifted, helped, encouraged, etc, then we are to do it, as we are to work together as a whole unit. We work together as a unit, helping each other grow, and be more fruitful. This is why it is important to listen to the Holy Spirit, guiding us and showing us who needs help, encouragement, etc. This is how I look at it. The roots are Jesus Christ. Without the roots, the tree is non-existent. Everything made from the tree, is only made through the existence of the roots. Hence, no Jesus = no tree. I think of the Holy Spirit as the sap. The sap runs through the tree and supplies what we need. He supplies gifts, prayer on our behalf, comfort, strength, fruits, protection, etc. When we share Jesus with others, our branches grow, and we are able as a whole, to produce more fruit. When we refuse to help those around us who need us, those branches begin to die, making the tree more bare. We want a full tree. The more branches, and the more fruit, the better. Therefore, we are to help everyone in need. If we help non-believers, our branches grow all the more, and our family of believers grow, producing more and more fruit as we add more branches. If we help those already on our tree, they are less at risk of a die off, and instead, grow more fruit. In other words, helping others, benefits our tree, hence, benefiting the kingdom of God.

We want our tree full, and we want our tree full of love. Love nurtures things and makes them grow. We don't add branches for our self benefit, but for the benefit of others, and ultimately, the kingdom of God. It is through that same love that Jesus showed us, that we want our tree full. Therefore, selfish intent is not what drives us, but instead, what drives us, is love. The love of Christ.

Ephesians 4:17-19-Ephesians 5:1-4

We, who are believers in Christ, should no longer be walking in a manner unworthy of our calling. We need to leave behind all foolishness, all malice, and all the things of the world. We need to adapt into our new self, which is the body of Christ. It is no longer I who live, but Christ in me. Therefore, we act as Christ would want us to act, we respond how Christ would want us to respond, and we walk, how Christ would want us to walk, by the Spirit.

The old self was corrupt, and in need of God's saving grace. Now that we have put off the old self, and went from flesh to Spirit, let us now live and walk by the Spirit, through Christ Jesus. By walking in the Spirit, we allow the Holy Spirit to move through us, unhindered, as He renews our mind, thoughts, and attitudes. This is done only through Christ Jesus. When we believed, we were born again, a new creation in Christ. This put on the new self, and rid us of the old one. The new man was created according to God, in true righteousness and holiness. Therefore, let us throw off everything that hinders, and keep our eyes on our race in God, through Christ Jesus.

Therefore we also, since we are surrounded by so great a cloud of witnesses, let us lay aside every weight, and the sin which so easily ensnares us, and let us run with endurance the race that is set before us, looking unto Jesus, the author and finisher of our faith, who for the joy that was set before Him endured the cross, despising the shame, and has sat down at the right hand of the throne of God.

For consider Him who endured such hostility from sinners against Himself, lest you become weary and discouraged in your souls.

Hebrews 12:1-3

And do not be conformed to this world, but be transformed by the renewing of your mind, that you may prove what is that good and acceptable and perfect will of God.

Romans 12:2

When we conform ourselves to Christ, instead of the world, we become more like Christ, and less like the world. This means that we have to die to ourselves, daily. This means that we are to leave behind the things that gratify the flesh, and yes, it may even mean leaving behind some of your hopes and dreams. Walking in the Spirit is not a one time thing. Walking in the Spirit means that you surrender daily, minute by minute, second by second. We leave behind the things of this world, to follow something greater, Jesus Christ. We love as Christ loves, we are kind as Christ is kind, etc. Therefore, we imitate God, and not the world. We walk in love, and we walk with Christ in the center of that love, the center of our life. This means that we put away things that don't belong in us. It could be cursing, talking foolishly, acting foolishly, etc. It can be the way that we think, it could be removing strongholds, etc. Instead of focusing on the things of the world, what should we be focusing on?

Finally, brothers and sisters, whatever is true, whatever is noble, whatever is right, whatever is pure, whatever is lovely, whatever is admirable—if anything is excellent or praiseworthy—think about such things. Whatever you have learned or received or heard from me, or seen in me —put it into practice. And the God of peace will be with you.

Philippians 4:8-9

Think about what we learned from Paul. He was a man who found Jesus, or rather Jesus found him, and Paul became born again, putting off his old self. His old self was corrupt, doing the things that his father taught him, instead of the things that God would want. Paul put his former self behind, and moved forward, becoming more and more like Christ. This was a choice. Yes, when we are born again, we are a new creation in Christ Jesus, but with that, comes the responsibility on our behalf, to walk as Jesus walked. It's a choice. A choice that we make daily, to follow the things of Christ, and not of the world. It's a choice, to surrender daily, take up our cross, and follow Jesus. Paul loved others, prayed for others, and became a new man, in Christ Jesus. Becoming a new creation, doesn't mean that things will automatically be easy for us. Scriptures don't tell us that our lives will be easy. In fact, we are told that in this world we will have tribulation, but to take heart, because Jesus overcame the world. So in scriptures, we see that Paul faced tribulations as well. For example, when Paul was imprisoned, among other times when he faced trials. We also see this in 2 Corinthians, when Paul expresses that he has a thorn in his flesh. He pleaded with God to remove it, but instead of getting exactly what he prayed for, God gave him what he truly needed. Paul needed to know that it is through his weakness, Christ's power will rest on him. Therefore, boast in those weaknesses, because when you are weak, then you are strong.

Therefore, in order to keep me from becoming conceited, I was given a thorn in my flesh, a messenger of Satan, to torment me. Three times I pleaded with the Lord to take it away from me. But he said to me, "My grace is sufficient for you, for my power is made perfect in weakness." Therefore I will boast all the more gladly about my weaknesses, so that Christ's power may rest on me. That is why, for Christ's sake, I delight in weaknesses, in insults, in hardships, in persecutions, in difficulties. For when I am weak, then I am strong.

2 Corinthians 12:7-10

This didn't mean that he rejoiced in the fact that the hardships gave him pain, on the contrary, he rejoiced in what those hardships produced in him. He rejoiced that through the pain, Christ's power made him strong.

Ephesians 5:8-10

Although you were once in darkness, you have now come into the light. We are to walk as children of the true light, Jesus Christ.

Then Jesus spoke to them again, saying, "I am the light of the world. He who follows Me shall not walk in darkness, but have the light of life."

John 8:12

You are all children of the light and children of the day. We do not belong to the night or to the darkness.

1 Thessalonians 5:5

As children of the light, we walk by the Spirit, and we find out what is good and acceptable to the Lord. We don't just find out what is good and acceptable, but we take action upon these things, and we walk in them.

Ephesians 5:15

Walk carefully. Do not walk as fools, but as wise, for the days are evil.

Ephesians 5:18

Those who are drunk with wine, allow the alcohol to control themselves. By drinking, you know that you are handing your whole self over, and giving your control over to the alcohol. Instead of being filled and drunk on wine, be filled with the Holy Spirit. Give your whole self to the Holy Spirit, allowing Him to be in control of you. God won't do it by force, it's a choice that you have to make. A choice to surrender the false sense of control that you are holding on to.

I want to add that this analogy can pertain to much more than wine. If you deal with anything in life, you can choose what you give the control over to. Take anxiety for example. I have been dealing with anxiety for years now. The anxiety was only able to have the hold over me that it did, because I gave in to it. I allowed the fear and anxious thoughts to rule me. I chose what I thought was the easy way out. I thought that if I gave in to every fear that came my way, then I wouldn't have to face anything that scares me. This however, only spiraled. The more I gave the fear control over me, the more it demanded. Eventually, the fear was so large, that it cast a shadow, and it felt so much bigger than what it truly was. Years later, I am still fighting the effects of this. I share this story, to tell you that whatever it is that is gripping you, whatever it is that is holding on to you, if you don't release it, and stop giving it control, it will only get bigger. Giving in to whatever it is that has a stronghold on you, never makes the stronghold go away. In fact, it only makes it grow so much bigger. And if you keep giving in to it, it will only grow bigger and bigger, until it feels like it's crushing you. Also, don't expect to just break a stronghold in a day, although anything is possible with God. Anticipate and prepare yourself for the battle ahead. Know that it may not be an easy one, but you can do it, because God is right there fighting with you and for you. You may have set backs, you may have moments of doubt, moments when that stronghold seems to be getting bigger, not smaller, etc. I had so many moments when I felt like I was taking 1 step forward, and 10 steps back. It felt as if fear was gripping me and I couldn't get it off. It was like a leach sucking me dry of every ounce of happiness that I had left, making me afraid of even leaving my room. And although through my eyes, at times it seemed as if nothing was changing, God knew better. God knew that if I kept pushing, it would eventually break. If I kept pushing, it would eventually get easier. It's been about 3 years or so of breaking this stronghold. It took a really long time to start seeing the change that the perseverance was producing in me. So please, don't give up. Even if it takes years, don't give up the hope that is within you. Keep having faith that God will answer your prayers. God does hear you. If God had made me instantly better when I asked, I would have never had the opportunity to go through this trial with Him. I would have never gotten to see all of the beautiful miracles, and all of the many ways that He picked me up, and encouraged me to keep going. And although this experience was one that hurt more than words could ever express, I am grateful at what it produced. It has shown me how truly good my Father really is. I have known God for as long as I can remember, but it wasn't until I faced a lot of really hard trials, that I got to know Him on a much deeper level than I ever would have without those trials. This came from multiple things. For example, me spending time with Him, in more than just prayer here and there. It was me reading, and truly getting to know how beautifully indescribable He truly is. How He carries me, even when I feel so numb that I can't even move. I have learned so much over these years, and even though they have been incredibly painful, they produced a result that was worth the pain. So please, don't give up. God does hear your cries for help. He hasn't forgotten about you.

Can a mother forget the baby at her breast
and have no compassion on the child she has borne?
Though she may forget,
I will not forget you!
See, I have engraved you on the palms of my hands;
your walls are ever before me.

Isaiah 49:15-16

This is how our beautiful God works, He turns the pain into a beautiful masterpiece, and He turns the mess, into a message. He turns mourning to dancing, and sorrow to joy. Wait for it, it will come. Anticipate it, and know that in His time, He is going to make all things beautiful.

I will turn their mourning into gladness;
I will give them comfort and joy instead of sorrow.

Jeremiah 31:13

You have turned for me my mourning into dancing;
You have put off my sackcloth and clothed me with
gladness,
To the end that my glory may sing praise to You and not
be silent.
O LORD my God, I will give thanks to You forever.

Psalm 30:11-12

Ephesians 5:22-31

I would like to add here some of what I wrote in my
Galatians bible study.

I feel the need to point something out. God does not love
men, more than women. We are all equal in God's eyes.
Gender, race, financial status, etc, do not affect God's
love for you.

Some women may wonder why husbands are the head of
the wife, or why men were mentioned so much in the
bible. You have to see that, woman were mentioned too,
however, there is an order of things. For example, the
order is that a woman should respect, and be submissive
to her husband. He is the head of the household. This

does not mean that God loves men more, it just means that there is an order of things.

Wives, submit yourselves to your own husbands as you do to the Lord. For the husband is the head of the wife as Christ is the head of the church, his body, of which he is the Savior. Now as the church submits to Christ, so also wives should submit to their husbands in everything.

Ephesians 5:22-33

Many of you may not like this, but this was God's design, not yours. We are in a society that says differently than what God says, therefore, passages like this, may make you question God's love for you, but don't. You are not loved any less than man. He made man with love, and He made you with that same love. Period.

You have to remember, that God made everything for its purpose, and there is an order in which things are created to be. If you see the passage after, we see that men have a part too.

Husbands, love your wives, just as Christ loved the church and gave himself up for her to make her holy, cleansing her by the washing with water through the word, and to present her to himself as a radiant church, without stain or wrinkle or any other blemish, but holy and blameless. In this same way, husbands ought to love their wives as their own bodies. He who loves his wife loves himself. After all, no one ever hated their own body, but they feed and care for their body, just as Christ does the church—

for we are members of his body. "For this reason a man will leave his father and mother and be united to his wife, and the two will become one flesh." This is a profound mystery—but I am talking about Christ and the church. However, each one of you also must love his wife as he

loves himself, and the wife must respect her husband.

Husbands, likewise, dwell with them with understanding, giving honor to the wife, as to the weaker vessel, and as being heirs together of the grace of life, that your prayers may not be hindered.

1 Peter 3:7

So many women get caught up in these verses, thinking that God must love men more, but you couldn't be farther from the truth. This verse below explicitly shows that we are all equally loved in God's eyes.

There is neither Jew nor Gentile, neither slave nor free, nor is there male and female, for you are all one in Christ Jesus. If you belong to Christ, then you are Abraham's seed, and heirs according to the promise.

Galatians 3:28-29

We have to stop going by the world's ideology of things, and start focusing on God's. Yes, God has an order of things, but this has nothing to do with God loving one more than the other. This is just how He made things to exist. Trying to change God's order of things, is like you trying to take a whale that lives in the sea, and make it live on land. It won't work, because God didn't design it that way.

Remember, He is the creator, not us.

All believers have the same redemption of sins, Jesus died for both men and women, we are all equally loved, and we all get to be with God one day. Focus on this, not the world's viewpoint.

And remember, God does not love men more than women, we are all equally loved.

Ephesians 6:1-4

This passage is for more than a child who is under age. Whether you are young or old, you should still honor your father and mother. There was no time limit placed on this, and this has nothing to do with how much they mistreated you as a kid, or how much they mistreat you now. The fact of the matter is, God never told us to honor our father and mother when they are nice to us, or when they treat us fairly. Instead, we are told honor them, period.

Fathers likewise, do not provoke your children to wrath. Bring your children up to honor the Lord. Teach them the truth, and teach them to respect and fear the Lord. This is good and pleasing to the Lord.

Ephesians 6:5-8

I would like to add that this may seem to be for people who were servants only, but if applied correctly, it means so much more than that. Whether it's your boss, or the president of the United States, we are being told to honor and be obedient to them, as if for the Lord. This means that if your boss yells at you, treats you harshly, or unfairly, our response should be the opposite. We should respond as if we were responding to the Lord, and not to man. The fact of the matter is, we are still servants of Christ. Therefore, we work as though everything we do is for the Lord. Serving Christ in all humility, love, and longsuffering. Knowing that we get our reward from Christ, and not from man. If man is mean to us, and we are mean back, what good is it? Does this make us more like Christ, or more like the world? If I am trading insults for insults, who am I pleasing? Myself, or the Lord? Therefore, everything that you do, do as for Christ, and let all that you do, be done with love.

Ephesians 6:9

Likewise, those who are bosses or have someone under them, be kind. Treat them fairly, knowing that you too have a Master in heaven, and there is no favoritism with

Him. And remember that with the same measure you use, it will be measured to you.

Do not judge, or you too will be judged. For in the same way you judge others, you will be judged, and with the measure you use, it will be measured to you.

Matthew 7:1-2

<u>Ephesians 6:10-13</u>

God holds the scepter of righteousness, and is the ruler of all. God rules over your enemies, over the darkness, and over all. Therefore, remember the strength of your God, and be strong in the Lord and in the power of His might.

Do not neglect to use the weapons of warfare that you were given. Put on the whole armor of God, for we do not fight with worldly weapons, but we stand and we fight with Spiritual ones. We fight with weapons that are not of this world. For how can we defeat what we can not physically see, unless we also use the weapons that we can not physically see? If you perhaps were to use a sword made by man, this would do nothing for your fight in the spiritual realm. We need weapons not of this world, to fight. For we do not fight against flesh and blood, although it may seem as if an individual is where our fight lies, it is actually a fight with something beyond that person. The person is like a puppet, used to tare you down, and make you lose your faith. However, as with a puppet, there is always someone holding the strings. You must look beyond the physical world, and look at the one pulling the strings. The enemy is the one who ultimately wants your demise. If the enemy can deter you from what God has planned for you, then he has succeeded in is his goal. Don't let him win the fight for your attention. Keep your eyes on Christ Jesus, and don't lose your focus. We can so easily be distracted by the things of this world, but you must remember that there is always something behind that person, that argument, and that fight. The enemy is the one with the strings, and we must know that he is present, in order to defeat him. If you are unaware that there is an enemy behind that distraction, then you are also unaware that there is even a fight that you need to be involved in. I believe that there is so much going on in the spiritual realm, and we can not see it with mere human eyes. Look at when Elijah prayed that his servant would see with spiritual eyes, what did he see? He saw an army surrounding them, ones that were fighting for them.

And when the servant of the man of God arose early and went out, there was an army, surrounding the city with horses and chariots. And his servant said to him, "Alas, my master! What shall we do?"

So he answered, "Do not fear, for those who are with us are more than those who are with them." And Elisha prayed, and said, "LORD, I pray, open his eyes that he may see." Then the LORD opened the eyes of the young man, and he saw. And behold, the mountain was full of horses and chariots of fire all around Elisha.

2 Kings 6:15-17

You must realize that there is a realm beyond what you can see. But, guess who can see it? God. This is why He so graciously gave us the tools to overcome what we can not clearly see. Because God loves us, and He wanted us to have protection against the things of this world. Things seen and things unseen. He gave us dominion over the enemy, over the unseen. We must be bold and brave, not in ourselves, but in Christ. Knowing that we have the Holy Spirit within us, and that nothing can overcome us, because of He who is on our side. Was it not the demons who were afraid of Jesus? Was it not the demons who begged Jesus? Was it not Jesus who silenced the demons? Why was this? Because they knew who He was, and they knew that He has all power and all dominion over them, and they still know it. Guess what? Those of you who are believers, you have that same authority. Jesus gave all that He has to us, and that includes the authority over the devil, demons, and whatever else may come against us. Because that's who we are in Christ. We are Jesus's warriors, and as Jesus's warriors, we conquer. Not because of our own strength, but because of the strength of Him who dwells within us.

When he arrived at the other side in the region of the Gadarenes, two demon-possessed men coming from the tombs met him. They were so violent that no one could pass that way. "What do you want with us, Son of God?"

they shouted. "Have you come here to torture us before the appointed time?"

Matthew 8:28-29

Moreover, demons came out of many people, shouting, "You are the Son of God!" But he rebuked them and would not allow them to speak, because they knew he was the Messiah.

Luke 4:41

However, when He, the Spirit of truth, has come, He will guide you into all truth; for He will not speak on His own authority, but whatever He hears He will speak; and He will tell you things to come. He will glorify Me, for He will take of what is Mine and declare it to you. All things that the Father has are Mine. Therefore I said that He will take of Mine and declare it to you.

John 16:13-15

And He said to them, "I saw Satan fall like lightning from heaven. Behold, I give you the authority to trample on serpents and scorpions, and over all the power of the enemy, and nothing shall by any means hurt you. Nevertheless do not rejoice in this, that the spirits are subject to you, but rather rejoice because your names are written in heaven."

Luke 10:18-20

No, in all these things we are more than conquerors
through him who loved us.
Romans 8:37

Ephesians 6:13

Therefore, we must take up our armor, and we must stand. We must fight against the enemy. Do not run in the face of fear, doubt, anxiety, and pain, instead, fight. Persevere, knowing that you have done all to stand.

Ephesians 6:14-18

Our armor has 7 pieces. These pieces are already strong, but so few of us know how to properly use them. This makes these pieces ineffective when you don't know how to wield them correctly. For instance, how can you use the sword of the Spirit to fight with the word of God, if you don't know the word of God? When the enemy attacks you with lies, how can you decipher the truth? When you have no faith that God will come through for you, how can you use the shield of faith? When you don't know the gospel, and you don't know about the peace that you were so graciously given through Christ, how can you walk in peace? If you don't pray, how can you effectively use the weapon of prayer? You must know what God has given you, and you must know how to use this armor correctly. Remember, we are not fighting with the weapons of this world, but Spiritual ones. Therefore, in order to fight effectively against things that we can not see, we need to know the word of God, we need to know who we are in Christ, we need to know that God has given us all of the tools that we need to defeat the enemy and His lies, etc. We were not left defenseless, and we were not left as orphans. We are told that He will never leave nor forsake us, and God does not lie. We were told that He is with us until the end of age, and God does not lie. We were told that we have all the power over the enemy, and God, does not, lie. You must believe this, and you must have faith. He who doubts is like the waves of the sea, they sway with every wind and every trial that comes there way. Instead, stand. Stand strong knowing who you are in Christ Jesus. Stand strong knowing that you can, and you will defeat the enemy. Stand strong knowing not only will you win the battle, but that God has already won the war. It's just a waiting game. Knowing that the enemy has already been defeated, and that soon enough the devil will end in the pit where he belongs. One day, we won't have to deal with his treachery, his lies, and his conniving self, but he will one day be no more. In the meantime, we fight. We fight knowing that the victory is already won, and Jesus already conquered all that needed to be conquered. And He gave us the tools to conquer in the meantime, while we wait the return of our beautiful Savior.

Ephesians 6:19-20

I pray for all believers, that we will boldly speak the truth. To be bold is not hesitating or fearful in the face of actual or possible danger or rebuff; courageous and daring. To be bold is someone who is not afraid to do things that involve risk or danger. To be bold is someone who is not shy or embarrassed in the company of other people. To be bold is to be courageous. I want to be bold. I want to speak the word of God with courage, and with boldness. We are ambassadors for Christ. We represent Christ, and I for one, want to represent Him without being timid, or fearful. I want to display myself as if I am displaying Christ, which as a believer, I am displaying Christ. I pray that you will join me in this prayer for all believers. We are ambassadors for Christ, let us boldly pronounce it.

Ephesians 6:23-24

Peace to the brethren, and love with faith, from God the Father and the Lord Jesus Christ. Grace be with all those who love our Lord Jesus Christ in sincerity. Amen.

Ephesians 6:23-24

<u>Bonus page</u>

You can not use Spiritual armor, if you don't have it. There is only one way to get it, and that's by believing in our Lord and Savior Jesus Christ.

Therefore, if you don't have Jesus, and you are trying to figure out why your equipping of armor is not working, this is the reason. It's because you don't have it.

You must believe in Jesus Christ, God's Son, in order for any of this to work.

Now I must add something. I don't believe in Jesus because of what He gives me. I do it, because I love Him. I have had the privilege of getting to know Him for so many years, and I have many reasons as to why I love Him so much, but I know that there may be someone who is reading this, who has not had this opportunity yet. However, I must tell you that Jesus has already shown you His perfect love. He has already shown you the greatest love that He could ever show you. How? He died for you. He took on your sin debt, and paid it in full. He did this for all who choose to believe in Him. So if you have been asking yourself why you should follow Jesus, and you have been wondering what's so different from other religions, I am here to tell you that there are many. But, before you even get to know the many reasons, the many things that make my Jesus so different, I share with you this one. This one that rings so true, that you lost your comparison right here. Jesus, who is God, came down in the flesh of a man, leaving behind His heavenly kingdom, just to redeem you. He came down, and He took on every single sin that you have and will ever commit, and took that sin on Himself, as if it was His. He died, paying what you owed. He died, redeeming your sins. He did this for all who choose to believe in Him. Why did He do that for you? Because He loves you. Meaning that if you choose to reject Him, then your sins have not been wiped clean, and you still owe a debt in which you can not afford. Based off of this information alone, why would anyone not want to follow such a merciful and gracious God? Why would anyone not want to follow someone who gave their life, just to save yours?

You can ponder this question, or you can make the choice that this is the God you stand behind. One who loves you unconditionally, despite all of your faults. When you choose to believe, and truly believe, all of the wrongs that you have ever committed, are wiped clean. When this happens, He looks at you and no longer sees your sins, but instead, all He sees is His love for you. God is not like anyone or anything that you will ever meet. There is none like Him. No one who would love you as much as He loves you, cares for you as much as He cares for you, and stands by you as much as He stands by you. He doesn't leave when things get tough, instead, He fights for you and with you. He can not be compared, because there is none to compare Him to.

If you have made the wonderful decision to follow Jesus Christ as your Lord and Savior, I will add a prayer below to help you start your journey. I know that sometimes it can be hard to find the words, so hopefully this helps.

I really hope that if you are someone who has been thinking about giving your life to Jesus, and are unsure, I hope that you don't ponder it too long. You never know the time or the day that your life will end. You could be young or old, death doesn't discriminate. You always have time to decide, until you don't. So don't wait, until it's too late.

Dear God,

I come to You today, recognizing that I am a sinner and in need of Your saving grace. I confess with my mouth that Jesus is Lord, and I believe that He died and You raised Him from the dead. You did this to save me. Thank You Jesus for loving me so much, that You gave your life to save mine. From here on out, I want to live my life for You, and only You. Help me live a life that pleases You. Thank You for all You have done for me. In Jesus name I pray, Amen.

If you prayed that prayer, I am so proud of you! The bible tells us that as soon as we accept Jesus, we are given the promised Holy Spirit. You now have the only One who can help you overcome this world, God Himself.

The journey may not be easy, but I promise you, it's worth it. The temporary trials of this life, could never outweigh the eternity that you will get to spend with a loving God, who calls you His child.

Welcome to our family.

To read more books by Tentmaker Ministries, please go to Tm-ministries.com

www.ingramcontent.com/pod-product-compliance
Lightning Source LLC
Chambersburg PA
CBHW011218120626
46545CB00008B/3049